I0617333

ON FATE

St. Albert the Great

Translated and Commentary by: D.P. Curtin

Dalcassian
Publishing
Company
PHILADELPHIA, PA

ON FATE *(de Fato)*

Library of Congress Cataloging-in-Publication Data

The Question of Fate: What is it? Is it a necessary force to impose order, and if so, what is its impact?

ON FATE *(de Fato)*

Section I:
Is there fate?

(1) Nothing is defined, unless it exists; fate for Boethius, is defined in *Consolation of Philosophy IV*; therefore it exists.

(2) Also, in the *De Generatione II* Aristotle says that each thing can be measured by a period of time; but the measure of the smallest of things, repeated over again in its metric, verifies its quantity.
If, therefore, the life of those who dwell below is measured by the circumference of a circle, which is called an epoch, it may be taken that the measure of a circle, by itself or equal to itself, is denoted by counting the life of those who abide below. Moreover, by the measurement of a circle, as distinguished by the twelve houses [of the Zodiac], it can be ascertained that similar things happen to those beings below as well. However, an epoch is not defined without the arrangement of the planets and the stars, and what events transpire because of their position and radiation. Therefore, from the heavenly spheres and their radiation, and their position in the heavens, they are known and numbered by those lives who dwell beneath them; and this is called 'fate'. Therefore, fate exists.

(3) Likewise, Aristotle says in *Physics IV* that to be in time is to be measured within a certain part of time. Now, since time is only a singularity, and it does not extend through a multitude of times, it is necessary that something can only be referenced in the context of the whole of time. However, this is nothing but the movement of the heavenly spheres. Therefore, by the movement of the heavenly sphere, the life of all beings below is caused and accounted for; and this is called fate. Therefore, it is peculiar, for the movement of these spheres, is as Aristotle says "like life to all things that exist".

(4) If by chance, a certain temperament is permanently fixed in the world below because of the celestial movements, then this is

surpassed by the volume of matter, and is therefore annulled. On the contrary: the lower material world is order to the one above- as matter is to its form, and as situated to its proper place, and as moved by their motions. Therefore, those things above move those below, and their formations, restraint and movement always triumph. All those beings which abide below are overcome and drawn to the arrangement of the heavens.

(5) If you say that it is true, in regards to these bodies, as St. Augustine appears to say in *City of God V*, that "starry breaths" can be said to apply to the transformation of even the bodies, but not to that of the soul[1]. On the contrary: the vegetative and intellectual powers of the soul do not function outside of the consonance of its own organ. If, therefore, consonance is governed by sidereal winds, the actions of the intellectual and vegetative soul will be regulated by those sideral winds.

(6) Further to this point, this appears to also be the case with the rational soul, as the philosopher says that our intellect is limited by time and space. However, time and space are perceived by both the senses and the imagination. Now, therefore, it has already been established that such things are subject to the influences of the stars, and by extension, the governance of the intellect.

(7) Again says the philosopher, that the soul is the instrument of the intellect, and that the intellect impresses upon it and illuminates it. Therefore, the intellect by its very movement creates the illumination within the intellectual soul. Yet, there is no middle ground between the mover and its motion, as Aristotle proves in *Physics VII*. Therefore, the intellect by its motion is nearest to the soul, or it is nearest to itself by conveying its cause to the soul through some other medium. Not by itself alone, as philosophically

---

[1] St. Augustine is famously critical of the claims of astrologers and their ability to make accurate predictions (Confessions, 5.3; 13.17).

speaking, the intellect is the engine of all things. It is necessary, therefore, that there should be some medium that would convey its illuminations to the soul. Yet, this method cannot be taken unless it is true that the motion of the air flows through, by its movement, those things which are below. Therefore, the intellect, through the movement of the heavens, regulates and is the force of causality behind the intellectual soul. We can see this analogically, for the heart, which according to Aristotle is "the point of origin for our senses, existence and vitality", does not implant these virtues into parts separate from itself, except by the instrument of the spirit; and so it is by all those things which move and are moved which are distant from each other. It will, therefore, be the same with the intellect and the soul, when the intellect lies at a distance from, yet impresses upon, the rational soul, as it lies in a secondary place which is still distant. It cannot be said philosophically that the intellect comes from those things below, as, according to the Philosopher, the intellect is in the world, and is cataloged among those things present in the world, or to the catalog of the rotations of the world, and by extension, to the movement of the world itself. As Aristotle says, [the world] is composed of the moving intellect and the celestial spheres, which also move.

(8) For the same reason, dreams of prognostication, as Macrobius says, whether they are oracles or reasoning or prophetic, are foretold in us[2], as Aristotle says in *De Somno et Vigilia, II*, by sign or cause or sheer chance; that is to say, an accident in the causal force itself, not a shared accident. Nevertheless, a dream is the passion of a dreamer. Therefore, through some sleep, a dream may take place to the sleeper. The occurrence of sleep, which can be a forecast of the future, cannot be caused by those things in matter, hot and wet, cold and dry. It must therefore be caused by some form, and which takes its form from the order and rule of those things below. This

---

[2] Albert appears to be referencing Macrobius' 'Dream of Scipio' which incorporated Roman astrology into its conception of human destiny.

form can only come from the movement of the heavens. Therefore, by the movement of the celestial spheres, something adheres to that below, by which the whole nature of life is governed. This is called fate, therefore, fate exists.

(9) Likewise, Ptolemy said that the elector is better than the prognostication, as he gains insights into the future from observing secondary stars. He calls secondary stars the efforts of stars that appear in the lower elements, within the clouds or their environs. From this we can deduce that the effects of the stars hold fast upon those beings below, from which knowledge of the future of life is caused and can be known. Now the mathematicians call this fate, therefore, fate exists.

(10) For that matter, Boethius in *De Consolatie Philosophe V* speaks of chance and fortune, which are caused by two causes in mutual confluence. For, just as when a man intends to dig up treasure and later another man intends to dig a grave in the same place, the discovery of treasure results from chance, and thus and therefore his fortune is caused by the two causes coinciding with themselves. As Boethius says that these "causes are brought together through the unity of the inevitable connection" of their causes, which "proceed from the source of premonition". A connection of this kind of cause is called fate by Boethius, therefore, fate exists.

(11) Boethius continues in the same place, saying that which foresees the chief lucidity of providence "destroys individual fates, and disperses them into places, forms and times." Therefore, fate exists.

(12) If it is said that fate is an order of divine premonition, then it does not contradict what has been stated. Since what this divine premonition has foreordained can be executed and completed through the ministry of natural causes, and to the explicit essential

order of things and to life from causes of this kind, which is called fate.

Counter-Argument

(13) St. Gregory in his homily on the Epiphany of the Lord said "Let it be far from the hearts of the faithful that something strange should be believed". He gives the reasoning as "because the stars were made for man, not man for the stars". If, then, the movement of the stars were the order of the livelihood of man, a minister would govern the life of the mast whom he services, which is incorrect.

(14) Just the same, St. Augustine, in his book *De Doctrina Christiana*, says that fate is nothing. Moreover, if mathematicians[3] can appear to foretell truths about the future sometimes, that this is achieved by the work of demons to deceive those unbelievers.

(15) Again, if there is a fate, it is caused by a cause. Not caused because it is regulated by fate, as the mathematicians say. Therefore, there will be causality. If the cause is either heavenly or earthly: not earthly because these things are hot, cold, wet or dry, wherein there is no sense of fate, nor heavenly, because those things above cause the movement of the celestial spheres, which mathematicians do not say it fate, but the cause of fate. Therefore, there is no fate.

(16) Just the same, those things which have nothing are twofold, as St. Augustine says. Namely, they derive from the first cause, which are life and light, neither of which is fate and in themselves. However, neither is the nature of a thing in itself fate, as the mathematicians claim, but rather is regulated by fate. Therefore, there is no fate.

---

[3] The use of the term 'mathematicians' here means something beyond its modern usage. Albert appears to be addressing the Pythagorian religious belief that 'all is number' in particular, a belief that is tied to conceptualizing the universe under strictly fatalist terms.

(17) Likewise, St. Augustine says that it is enough for those who dwell below to say that the will of God is the force of causality, as all things take place either by the will of God or by God's permission. Yet, the will of God is not fate. Therefore, it is nothing in itself.

(18) Likewise, everything that has existence maintains a state of order, as Boethius says. Yet, fate does not maintain order, as we see the unworthy exalted and the worthy cast down, which is shambolic. Therefore, when fate is supposed to be arranging such things, fate appears to be nothing.

(19) Moreover, if fate is an effect of the celestial spheres, those things which are of one of those spheres appear to be of one date. Yet, Jacob and Esau, "conceived from one intercourse with Isaac, our father"[4], are of the same sphere and yet they were not of the same destiny, as later events would indicate. Therefore, it appears that fate is nothing. [5]

---

[4] See Genesis 25:24

[5] Ymarmenen appears to be an attempt to converge and Latinize the Greek words 'μοίρα' and 'πεπρωμένο'. It appears nowhere else beyond its use by Albert.

Section II:
What is fate?

It is further asked what is fate.

(20) Boethius says in *De Consolatione Philosophiae* that "fate is the disposition inherent in movable things, by which providence binds each thing to its order."

(21) Hermes Trismegistus[6] says that fate, which the Greeks call 'ymarmenen' is the confluence of causes temporarily distributed to each man and woman, which have been preordained by the mystery of the heavenly gods.

Solution:

Firstly, fate is spoken about in many ways. Fate is sometimes said to be the timeliness of death, as it is said in Anticlaudianus[7], "livor[8] rests after fate". In this way Plato ascribes the course of life to the three deities of fate, namely to that of Clotho and Lachesis, who offer progress, and Atropos, who gives conclusion. As it is said "Clotho holds the strainer, Lachesis draws, Atropos kills". And here, because of this, we do not ask of fate.

(20) Secondarily, fate is said to be a disposition towards divine providence about those things taking place in the future, in the progress and the life of those below. Since this is an eternal disposition, it does not take place in the thing itself, but only when the effect is explained, then that effect is taken in by things and fulfilled in their correct time and place. Just as the preordering and predetermination of someone's perception of his own personal

---

[6] This is a relatively strange source for a medical scholastic author (and especially a Doctor of the Catholic Church) to draw from, as Hermetic texts, such as those allegedly written by Hermes Trismegistus were often deemed heterodox. This is perhaps why there is a tradition which falsely associates Albertus with various ventures into Occult knowledge.

[7] This is a relatively obscure work by Alain de Lille, the French theologian and poet from the University of Paris. Among scholastics he is one of the few scholars interested in Aristotle prior to the work of Albert.

[8] A skin discoloration or bruising that takes place after death

conduct places within them a message, but puts nothing in that message. Yet, it is nevertheless fulfilled by the message, when he directs it makes it part of his own conduct. And in this way Boethius in *De Consolatione Philosophiae* speaks of fate. And in this way, yet again, we do not inquire here about fate. However, the fundamental nature of this preordination, which exists in the mind of God, is simple, divine, eternal, immaterial, and unchangeable, yet it is formed through temporal things. It, therefore, becomes temporal and material and a multiplicity, changeable and conditional.

(21) Thirdly, fate is said to be the fundamental nature of order and the life of those who abide below, caused in them by the movements of the celestial spheres, whose radiance they are surrounded by at birth. In this same manner, Hermes[9] speaks of fate, calling the gods stars and the mystery of the godhead immoveable and the life of those who abide below. Now this fundamental nature is not its innate state, but rather the nature of a certain universal and ontological order, and of life itself, simple in essence, multitudinous in power. It has the simplicity of its own essence from the ordinary rotation of the common circle. Yet, it has a multiplicity of power from the many things contained in the circle. For this flows from many stars, from places and images, from radiance and conjunction, and from prohibitions and the multiplicity of angles. This is described in the intersection of the rays of the heavenly bodies and in the rays produced in the center above, in which alone, according to Ptolemy, all the powers of those in the celestial spheres are gathered together and united. Yet, this fundamental nature is a middle ground between the necessary and the uncertain. Whatever may be necessary in the movement of the celestial spheres is necessary, but whatever may be uncertain and changeable is a part of the generally corruptible and material world. Now this state, which is caused by the celestial spheres and yet inherently corruptible, is the medium between the two states. Everything

---

[9] Again referring to Hermes Trismegistus

proceeds forth from a noble cause to an ignoble cause, while it retains the property of that cause in itself, it also has its own being, except so far as the subject permits this to be the case. For everything that is received, as Boethius and Aristotle says in *Ethics VI*, is so in that which it is received, according to the power of the receiver and not according to the power of the cause from which it originates. We can observe this in what is called by Dionysius[10] the divine processions -- such as life and reason and wisdom and the like, which so far as they proceed away from God into our own world, become more temporal and changeable and mixed into material power and privation. Yet, they are still in God, simple and eternal, immutable and immaterial. The same is true, therefore, of the form by which the order of the world is assigned, which within the celestial sphere is necessary and unalterable. That inalterability is present in all created things, which because of the transience of their own existence, is received with both contingency and transience. Thus Boethius in *De Consolatione Philosophiae* proposes many circles, the center of which is the pivot and cause of fate and destiny. In the first circle of the center is the immutability of fate, which is referential to its cause, and in the far circle, in which the same generable and corruptible things of the same fate are also contained, there is the contingency and transience of all things created and their corruption. And so the nature of being and life is centered in the mind of the first mover. The circle close to the center is the same order of arrangement as it is in that celestial place, but the circle distant from the center observes the same order of arrangement, as it is transiently attached to created and corruptible things. Now this form, since it is in the image of time, potentially and virtually prefigures the wholeness of being and function of the lifetime of those created and corrupted. And so, although it is necessary from necessity, it is still transient and contingent. The cause of which is best assigned by

---

[10] Dionysius referenced here is Dioynsius the Areopagite, the Neo-Platonist author of the 5th century, a work of pseudepigrapha assuming the name of an Apostle of St. Paul.

Ptolemy in the Quadripartite[11], who says that the virtues of the stars are by one thing, and by chance reproduce by those below. Indeed by another, for through the sphere of those things active and passive, active and passive quality are passed to those below. By chance, when this form flows from a necessary and immutable cause, it happens to have its being in contingent and transient things. Therefore, it derives its transience from two things, namely the quality of the elements, that which it is brought to be created, and from the being of the created in which it is the subject. So this is then fate.

(1) And we, therefore, agree with the first reason, as we grant that this is the way that it should be.

(2) And in this same way, we grant the second reason that things are measured by time.

(3, 4) Now, to what is stated thirdly and fourthly that those below are indeed born to obey those above. Yet, those below and above are related to each other in two ways. If the relationship is present in a single simple form, which those things above give and those below receive, then it is true that the mover above is necessarily moved by those below. Moreover, perhaps this is the relationship between those things above and those things below which are movers of the celestial orbs. Yet, if the lower mover is in the one form, which it does not receive from that above, but is self-referential as directed by itself and its instrumentation, then nothing prevents it from being hindered by the opposite of its form or by some other temperament, so that it does not receive its motion from those things above. Therefore, it is hot and cold in relation to the virtues of heavenly things. For it is hot by its true form, not its celestial, and is the totality of homogeneity and the separation of heterogeneity, and cold is its opposite. And these qualities, through the contrariety found in the material world and the diversity of the temperament of matter, regularly exclude the effects of celestial

---

[11] A book specifically about the influence of stars on human behavior

movements. For this reason, Ptolemy says that a wise man rules the stars. Whereas the Commentator[12] says that the effect of the celestial spheres are on minor humors and disposes the body to the quartana[13]. The wise physician foreseeing this, through warm and moist bodies, is disposed to the blood, and then excludes those celestial effects, when the quartana is not induced.

(1) To what is further objected, we must answer that in this way the constitution of the vegetative and sensible virtues are alluded to as fate. However, since the disposition of fate is excludable and preventable from its own opposite discoverable in matter, then it is also excludable from its opposite found in the sensible soul. For they do this with the apprehension of the sensible soul, which is accomplished through the temperament of both activity and passivity in bodies. When conceived by the imagination of a woman, the whole of the body is transformed into a venereal[14] one. For this reason Avicenna said that some people became lepers from their imagination of leprosy[15], and Galen prohibits the flow of blood suffering from the appearance of red spots. If, therefore, the opposites of the celestial movements are understood, its effect is removed, just as it is removed from the body by opposite disposition[16]. Yet, by bodily temperaments and the apprehension of animals, appropriate to the celestial movements, this celestial effect is aided. This is, therefore, what Messehallach[17] calls the celestial effect, which he says is "winged" and is assisted by a wise

---

[12] This is presumably the 2nd century Roman physician Claudius Galen to whom he is referring, who makes commentary on earlier Hippocratic Medicine.

[13] Something that takes place every four days, usually associated with a fever or sundry medical symptom.

[14] Venereal is the truest sense of the Latin word. That is belonging to Venus, ergo related to both romance and sex.

[15] Avicenna speculated in his medical writings that the appearance of leprosy was an affliction not just the skin but of the whole body and of the soul.

[16] This is the basis for Hippocratic Medicine's theory of Allopathic treatment.

[17] This appears to be the awkward Latin transliteration of the name Masha'allah, as in Mashallah ibn Athari, who was a Jewish-Persian astronomer of the 9th century who wrote frequently on the science of the judgment of the stars.

astronomer, just as with those terrestrial things he is assisted by plowing and sowing.

(8) To what is being objected to concerning the cause of dreams, it seems to me to be obvious, especially concerning dreams which are caused by imaginary visions.

(7) To what is being objected to concerning the illumination of the intellect within the rational soul, according to philosophy it is answered in two ways: In the first way, according to the Stoics, who held that every noble substance has by command to move those below, and those below obey it. For just as the soul is fascinated by one thing, seeing the other hinders it and confabulates its operation. For they say that by virtue of some force from above, either by the intellect or by a star, the soul of one is elevated to a higher degree, and another to that of a lower degree. Therefore, the lower is born to be changed by the understanding of the higher, and thus to become fascinated. As Aristotle said, that there is no middle between the mover and the moved, it is not said to be always understood in terms of immediacy of place or space, nor of the immediacy of a higher or lower degree, setting it as an example of what came before. It is because the organ of imagination[18] is not immediate to the seed-vessels[19], but born in the image of a woman, and as such the seed-vessels are extended and flow in because of the immediacy of those things above and below, which is between the one ordering them and that whom it is ordered. Therefore, according to the opinion of the Peripatetics[20], it does not agree well, because without any doubt there must be an immediacy of union and contact between the agent,

---

[18] The phrase 'organ of the imagination' is an interesting one, as it appears to be drawn from various phraseologies in late antiquity. Aristotle considered that imagination (phantasia) to be a function of the soul, independent of perception. This appears to be the point of origin of faculty psychology, which Albert would have been familiar with, as it hit its apex during the medieval period.

[19] Interestingly enough this term has survived in modern science, but only in the field of botany, where it refers to the ripened wall of a plant ovary.

[20] A lesser known school of Aristotelian philosophy from Athens. More likely than not, Albert is taking this from the writings of Theophrastus, whose works only began to recirculate in the Latin West in Albert's lifetime.

the mover, and its motion. For this reason, we say that just as digestive heat has both double power and only one power, insomuch as the heat of a fire can be one thing, which can alter separate things into different kinds and cook it and do other things, inasmuch as it is the instrument of the soul (which is the beginning of life) according to which it ends its life by digesting it into all the forms of those things that live, so also is the celestial movement of the double power. In one way, as the movement of a body is circular and as such it moves bodies. In another way, as it is an instrument of moving intelligence, it affects the sensible soul by forms of bodies and the intellectual soul by forms of illuminations. For, as we have said, the forms which are made within someone are made in him according to the power of the receiver and not within the power of the giver.

Whatever else might be objected to in this part is plain.

(13) To what St. Gregory said, it must be said that he himself speaks of fate, according to the fact that some philosophers and heretics were said to impose necessity on certain things, just as the poet Paris[21] said: "Your destinies drag you, so that you can never leave the beginning."

(15) To what is asked, whether fate is the cause or the caused, it must be said that there is a similarity between the cause of the whole order of life and being, and thus there is something of a cause, although it is not a true cause. Inasmuch as it adheres to created things, it is a caused temperament, although it expresses the likeness of the cause. For as a form it contains the contents of life, both moving and contingent.

(19) To what is objected to about twins, we must say that although it is during intercourse the seed is thrown out in turn and in turn swallowed by the mother, so that there is not one hour for the

---

[21] Albert here is citing not another author, but the fictional voice of Paris of Troy from Virgil's *Aeneid*. He uses this same quotation elsewhere in his work *De Quindecim Problematibus*.

conception of twins. For if we assume them to be conceived in the same hour, they would share the same heart, from which they would be formed together and not as one. And when that center is changed, the whole of the circle must be changed, and thus their vista is not the same, nor are the angles the same, nor are the arrangement of the house [of the Zodiac] the same. And thus the whole of time is made different, and as a consequence of this, adheres to all things born, the varied temperament of fate is therefore necessary in its variety.

And by this the solution to the things that were asked are clearly articulated.

(16-18) Others are clear, and by themselves, obvious to everyone.

Section III:
Whether it imposes necessity on things

Consequently, it is asked whether it imposes necessity on things.

(1) It appears so. For whose cause is necessary, he is also necessary. Yet, the cause of fate is by the celestial sphere, which is necessary. Therefore, fate is both necessary and imposes necessity onto things.

(2) Just the same, fate is the measure and rule of all existence and life, but these necessary regulations refer to the rule, yet the rule is necessary. Therefore, it appears that fate imposes necessity on fatal things.

(3) Likewise, those above are stronger than those below. Therefore, those above necessarily draw those below to their own disposition. Yet, since fate is the bond by which things below are drawn to things above, it will be seen that fate imposes necessity on things.

(4) Likewise still, Aristotle said that harmony between the motions above and below is true harmony, just as with the chords of the lyre. Yet, for harmony to be it is necessary that those below should in all things achieve the constitution of those above. Therefore, the arrangement of those things above adhering to those below imposes a necessity upon them.

Counter-Argument:

Fate is bound to the motion of things, as was said before, and arrives through their own movability. However, it is exactly in their movability that those things are moved. Therefore, it relates contingently to things and does not impose necessity.

Solution:

It must be said that fate can be changed for many reasons, as we said before. Therefore, it imposes no necessity on things, but inclines to those heavenly things if there is not an opposite disposition stronger in material which is moving to the contrary.

And hence, Aristotle attributes these kinds of motions to joint counsel in *De Somno et Vigilia*, for certain reasons wise counselors suggest that something should be done advantageously. That, however, those below dissuade those who meet with difficulty, and thereafter the law of wise counsel is dissolved. And so it is said, that the counsels of the wise are often changed by the counsel of others; for the rule of Lesbia's[22] building is changed once built, as Aristotle says. But Lesbia is an island[23] on which the stones are not bent to a straight line, and therefore it is necessary that the rule according to which they are bent towards the buildings themselves. And so it is ontologically and the life of those below, in which, due to material causes, the state of the wise celestial circle often changes, and the state itself, which adheres to those moveable things, which is called fate. This deviates beyond the straightness of the celestial spheres and becomes large because of the many transformations of the opposites of those below.

(1) To the first question, that if the cause of fate is necessary -- but it does not follow from this except that it is itself necessary, because it does not adhere to them according to the power of heavenly things, which are necessary, but according to the power of those below, which is entirely changeable and transient.

(2) To the second reply, the relationship that exists between the ruler and the governed is as necessary as the relationship between father and son. Yet, since the change causes relationships and also the destruction of relationships, therefore, the changes which are in moveable things are the cause, and those regulated do not follow the rule, and this respect is unregulated.

(3) To the third reply, although those above are stronger than those below, yet it is because of the impotence of those below that not all

---

[22] Lesbia was the literary pseudonym used by the Roman poet Gaius Valerius Catullus who wrote in the 1st century BC. Albert is perhaps conflating this work of pseudepigrapha with the broader corpus of the works of Sappho of Lesbos, who wrote several centuries earlier.

[23] Albert is perhaps confused with the island of Lesbos which is in the Aegean sea.

things can achieve the effects of those above. And as to this, the bond is released on their part.

(4) To the fourth answer, that the solution of the control of things introduces dissonance in the guitar. The change and alteration of those things that are below causes dissonance from those things above. Therefore, Damascenus[24] says that those above are definitive signs to those below, but they are in no way the cause of our action.

---

[24] The Latin transliteration of 'Of Damascus', almost certainly the Syriac hymnographer John of Damascus who wrote in the 7th century. His citations here is curious, as the corpus of his works were well known in the Latin west (being that he is a doctor of the Catholic Church), as his astronomical teachings were considered doctrinally suspect shortly after his death.

Section IV:
Whether fate can be known

Consequently, it is asked whether fate is knowable.

(1) And it appears not, since it is the effect of the celestial spheres and a certain resemblance, just as the form of some order is similar to the cause of the same order -- and in the celestial sphere as far as we are concerned to be considered infinite, as the stars in number and kind and virtues, and as their position in the inclined circle, and outside it, and the distances and conjunctions, and the quality of the angle of under which the ray indicates, and the part of fortune, and the degrees of light, and shade in the wells, and existing in towers, and the like below as far as we are concerned. It will also be seen that its effect cannot be known to us.

(2) Likewise, the circle contains the giver of life, and the giver of fortune, and the giver of sense and understanding, which is called Hyleg and Alchochoden[25] by Mathematicians. Otherwise, it would not be the measure of the whole of life, because it would not include the principle of life. For the hour that is the beginning of all hours is the hour of the fall of the seed into the womb. Yet, as far as we are concerned, we cannot know this. Therefore, the form of the arrangement of all life will be unknown, and thus the fatal arrangement of all things will be unknown.

(3) And this is seen from the results. For there are some which seem to have one function, and yet they are accidents in and of themselves. For as there are male and female, which are not the same, for the cause of this cannot be known from the effect of the celestial spheres.

---

[25] These are terms taken from the realm of classical Greek astrology. Hyleg is the planet which is the strongest on the birth chart. It appears to be derived from the Arabic word for 'giver for life', as noted by Albert. The Alccochoden is its bound ruler. Albert appears to be familiar with both of these terms, but does not appear to endorse that they are instrumental in effectively making any predictive statements.

(4) It is the same, for those that are born in the eighth month, as they die more frequently, and those born in the seventh month live.

(5) Similarly, in twins, one of which is male and the other female, it very rarely happens that the male survives, but the female sometimes survives. And the cause of these is either impossible or very difficult to assign to the celestial spheres.

(6) Likewise, if Mars radiates enmity with those luminaries existing in the head of Algol[26] or the Gorgon[27], then the child, as Ptolemy says, will have his hands and feet cut off, and the cut limbs will be hung on the cross.

(7) Likewise, concerning what he says, that when the moon is in Leo, you should not put on new clothes, for it is very difficult to find a reason from the celestial spheres. If such conclusions were knowable, they would be directed to these principles from which the syllogism can be concluded. From this, there can be no way to reason, for it does not follow. The moon is in Leo, therefore it is bad to put on new clothes. Or, there are luminaries in the head of Gorgon, and the hostile radiation of Mars faces them from the square or from the opposite diameter. Therefore, the child will then be hung on the cross.

Solution:

It should be said that there are two parts to astronomy, as Ptolemy says: it is one of the superior positions and their quantities and their proper passions, and this is determined by observation. There is another matter of the effects of the stars in the lower world, which are received transiently in changeable things. Therefore, this is not determined except by conjecture, and the astronomer is incorporated into those things physically, and must be construed from physical signs. Yet, conjecture, since it is based on transient

---

[26] Known colloquially as the Demon Star, a bright multiple star in the constellation of Perseus.

[27] A vicious female monster from Greek mythology with sharp fangs and hair of living, venomous snakes.

signs, generates an attitude of less certainty than that of knowledge or opinion. For since such signs are common and transient, syllogism cannot be derived from such signs, for they do not include what was signified in most cases. Yet, as far as it can be known, there are judgments that are transient for many reasons, as it is clear from the aforementioned. And therefore, the astronomer often speaks the truth and yet what he says does not come to pass, since what he speaks is the truth in regard to the order of heavenly things, but this order is excluded from the transience of things below.

(1) To the first answer, there are many things to be considered, and as far as we are concerned, these considerations are few in number to which other things obey. And from this, the conjecture made is considered to be predictable. For this reason Ptolemy says, that the elector only makes judgment by probability and commonality, that is to say, by higher common cause, which the proper cause of things very often excludes.

(2) In addition, this hour is difficult to know, and therefore, a remedy can be taken towards the ascending steps of the secret. That is to say, it is the hour or union or prevention, the luminary is equaled by the circle, because it influences every birth that follows. Or, it may be taken ascending to birth from the womb.

(3) Additionally, a conjectural conclusion can be known through syllogism. Yet, the imperfection of knowledge does not prevent, as Ptolemy says, the extent of knowledge of knowable things. This is the same with the prediction of dreams. For there is no syllogistic relationship between the dream image and the interpretation of the dream. And so, it is all conjectural opinions.

(5) Regarding the disparity of the sex in twins, we must say that the female sex always occurs through the occasion of the lack of some principle. For since the seed of men is active and formative through the constructive power which is self-contained, it always brings forth the male form through its own intention, unless it is hindered by the quality of the material and therefore indicates the female sex from a

defect[28], and no particular nature intends to form a female. Yet, since this cannot be done better from universal nature, it becomes a generation and not properly generated, for this is a woman. This is what the Lord intends to say in Genesis 2: 18, "it is not a good man". That is to say, for "a man to be alone. Let us make him a helper like himself". Hence the disparity of the sex in twins results from the lack of natural principles on the reverse side of the seed and not from the epoch of celestial time. Yet, in such twins the male child often dies. This takes place because one twin is born from one divided seed. It was a matter of badly being terminated by that formative power. Yet, if it had been possible of being terminated, both would have been formed into a sea. Yet, the matter of the male needs a larger and stronger termination than that of a woman. Therefore, the male remains sick and weak, and life's terminates because of the matter of the woman and its cause. Yet, the woman, for whom a small termination suffices, sometimes survives because of the elasticity of the older body. However, most often, both die.

(4) To what is rejected about the eighth month, some have falsely said commonly those born in the eighth month die. For the eighth month is attributed to Saturn, whose cold and drought kill those born. So that this is proved false by the fact that many in astronomy are said to be sons of Saturn, who abide for a long period of time. The cause then is not in the celestial movements, but in natural principles. For the moon maintains greater dominance, by whose revolutions conceptions and pregnancies are measured, as Aristotle says. For the moon is another sun, in that it receives the light of the sun; and what the sun does in a year, the moon does in a month. From its beginning until it is half-way through, it is hot and humid as it is in springtime. From midday to full moon, it is hot and dry as it is in the summer. From the full moon to the second half moon, it is cold and dry like autumn. And from the second meditation to its

---

[28] This comically sexist statement by Albert is not his alone, or rather, he is not the progenitor. It is derived from Galenic medicine which posited this medical theory during Roman antiquity. This remained a medical precept until the Renaissance of the 15h century with the rise in the study of human anatomy.

full conjunction it is cold and wet like the winter. And that she[29] was born to move the humors is evident from the approach and retreat of the sea[30]. For if the flow of the sea be the smallest, it will return to the same point of smallness on the fourteenth day. For although the moon in the middle of its cycle passes only half way, the motion of the moon, meeting from its opposite side, completes its own rotation. For the moon is twice in the waxing in each given month. That is, in procession and conjunction with the sun. For the moon in conjunction receives light giving light from the sun; and since Venus is never far from the sun, and Venus has to move in the seminal moisture, when the moon is joined to the sun, it thereby acquires the power of Venus. And so by virtue of his[31] own power, he moves the humors, by the power of the sun he infuses life into the humors, and by the power of Venus he moves the seed of each generation according to the forms of generations. And because Mercury is also with the sun, Mercury has the power of mixing from its many revolutions, which it has more of than any other planet. The moon, therefore, earns its power from its union with Mercury, and from that union it moves the seed of man and woman into conjunction. Thus, the moon by its revolutions causes and regulates confluence, conceptions, and impregnations. Now there are seven necessary changes in every generation -- the first of which is the conversion of the seed, and particularly to the shape of the heart, to which everything else is formed. Second is the distinction of matter to the form of the principal components, which also have creative virtues, as the liver creates natural virtues, and the brain animal virtues, the seed vessels the formative virtues of conceptual things.

---

[29] Here Albert personified the moon as a woman, which is perhaps true to its Latin roots, wherein the lunar deity Selene was venerated into late antiquity. Or perhaps, in a more cosmogenic sense, as the roman deity Luna, who was said to be the consort to Sol, god of the sun. In either case, lunar activity is associated with the feminine in the Latin world well into the medieval period.

[30] That is to say, the movement of the tides twice daily.

[31] This change in pronoun appears to be intentional, as Albert is now speaking of the sun as its subject. This is perhaps confusing to a lay reader, as its personification is implicit and not explicit.

And therefore, from the second change adhere to the point of the heart three vesicles, which the spirit brings to the place where the brain, the liver, and the seminal vessels are. The third change is the distinction of matter, when the bladder of the brian ascends upwards, and the bladder of the liver a little lower to the right, and the bladder of the seminal vessels descends last. This descent and ascent is affected by the exaltation of the spirit which abides in the heart. The fourth change is the separation of the whole matter, so that it may be redistributed to the places of the secondary members, which do not have creative powers. By this distinction it is again made by the exhalation of the heart. This exhalation both penetrates and extends the matter, and by penetrating the material it makes the path of the veins pulsate, and become dormant, and nervous, and by stretching it distributes the matter to each member to its proper place. The fifth change is in the transmutation of matter into the shape of limbs, which shape it would not have received unless it were moist, and this change is effected by the formative force of the heart driven into the place of the limbs by the exhaled breath. Yet, the formed members are not fit to receive the power of motion and operation, except through confluence and binding, which are completed by the sixth change through the heat of the heart and the spirit diffused into its members, which by drying the surplus moisture combines and strengthens the joints and connections. In the seventh change, movement flows from the heart into all the members through the motivating virtues. Yet, since every movement of birth is from the moon, as has already been said, it must be completed by the seven revolutions of the moon in man, who is the most perfect animal. And although these changes of the seed do not take place successively according to the number of months, yet their completion does not take place until after the complete number of conversions according to seven months; and in other animals these are not so regularly observed by man, on account of the inferiority of their complexions, but some are pregnant for a longer time like elephants, others in a shorter time. And when these seven conversions of the seed have been completed, the embryo has what is required for survival. But, as Galen says, formative power has a threefold relation to matter; for sometimes matter is diminished and virtue abundant, sometimes they are proportioned according to equality, sometimes virtue is deficient and matter superabundant. And when, indeed, virtue is abundant and the material is diminished, it is terminated in the seventh month; and then the abounding power makes a strong movement to exit, and a child is born and grows strong and becomes small in body and very agile in operations. Yet, when strength and matter are adequate, and when there is a superabundance of matter, then it is not completed in the seventh month, but rests during one revolution of the moon, which is the eighth month, and when it is completed in the ninth month, it makes a movement towards the exit, and is born in the ninth month and then recovers. This, as in most cases, is the birth of all mankind. However, if there is a deficient power due to the disobedience of matter, out of distress it makes a movement in the seventh month, when the power of motion is given, and because of its deficiency it does not complete itself until the eighth month, and then it is born and dies in most cases. This does not occur out of time, but from the corruption of natural principles. Now these things which have been said are true in most cases; for the constitution of women and the constitution of the climate make a great deal of variation. Because of this, I saw one who gave birth in the eleventh month to a child of the greatest size. Aristotle says that he saw one which gave birth in the fourteenth month.

(6) To what is objected about being born on the head of a Gorgon, it must be said that those stars are funerary and indicate the monstrous termination of life. For which reason, even Perseus himself holds this severed head with his face turned away. As such, as we said before, it does not impose a necessity on things, but an easily malleable propensity.

(7) The same solution is wearing new clothes and the moon being in Leo. For just as the radiation of time impresses the arrangement of

order and duration upon natural things, so it impresses it upon artificial things.

(8) Because of this, the figures of magical images are ordered to be made to look at the stars.

Section V:
In What Kind of Case Fate Falls

Now what is being asked, in what kind of cause fate itself falls, has already been resolved by the prior antecedents. Yet, since there is no true cause, there is still something of the cause. For it is the form of the order of being and of life, having the image of the heavenly spheres of virtues. As we also sometimes say, that some are not really beings or non-beings, but they are some kind of being, such as those which are in the soul, and according to certain movements and time, as Avicenna says.

(1) Some, however, endeavor to prove that it is a cause, by what Plato says, comparing the stars to those things which are born, in which there are forms, which are the causes of generated things and the rule of being and of their life. For Plato brings forth the god of gods speaking to the corporeal gods, who are the stars, and saying: "Of these," that is to say, those born in the lower realm, "I will make seed and hand it over to you; it will be yours to carry out the match." And he asks them what they should see in nature, similar to themselves, and that they should worship piety and love justice. They take "this" to themselves after the dissolution of earthly ties, understanding "this" of pious men, which is immortal in their understanding. And after death, receiving the starry seats, as from the seed one descended into generations of stars. Because of this Plato also said, that descending through the spheres of the planets one receives the powers of the soul, memory, intelligence, and will, and the like, just as Macrobius explains in *On the dream of Scipio*.

(2) This also seems to be touched on by Ovid speaking of the milky circle and saying: "This is the way above to the great thundering roofs."

(3) This can also be seen by reason, because of those whose essential act is one, their nature seems to be one. Yet, the heavenly and human intelligence in the conception of truth seem to be one essential act, therefore belonging to one nature.

(4) And still further, whatever forms have one nature, they have one relationship to the body of one nature, if they are said to be in any body. Yet, the relation of celestial intelligence is to a star or to an orb comparable to itself. Therefore, the relationship of the intellectual nature in man will be comparable to a star.

(5) This is also seen by the statement of the Commentator[32] in *Metaphysics XI*, where he says that the end of the prosperity of man's intellect is if it continues after death in the celestial engine.

Solution:

It must be said that it is false and heretical to say that the intellectual soul descends from a star. For this was the opinion of the Egyptian philosophers[33], that the intellectual souls, made in the stars by the god of gods, are weighed down by the earthly affection with which they are sometimes affected; and that gravity brings down generable and corruptible bodies. Purified by the same, through the worship of piety and justice, they are received back to the stars. They said that the earthly affection reaches the intellectual soul in the same way that the soul is affected by the sweetness of the nourishment of the body. For it is posited that the bodies of the planets are nourished by the very fine vapor of the Maeotid[34] marshes. They are situated between the two solstices, between which is the greatest movement of the planets, so that when they attract it by gravity they are depressed and pushed back, and when they build up the same, they are raised and directed by their speed. This subtlety in the sphere of fire and air they called "the nexus of the gods". And in this way, they said that the affection of the earth reaches the souls placed in the stars. So that the heretics, seizing the opportunity of error from this opinion, said that all the souls

---

[32] That is to say, Aristotle

[33] It is unclear where Albert is getting this concept, perhaps from medieval texts on hermeticism. However, Ancient Egyptian religion did endorse that the Akh, the intellectual soul, was created in the stars.

[34] Maetid or Maeotians, were an ancient people dwelling along the Sea of Azov. Since this is a region known for its fog, it is presumed that this is the intention of the 'very fine vapor'.

are made in heaven with the angels, because of the sin they committed, were cast into these earthly bodies, that they might be received here again purified to the heavenly seats. For this is what David says (Ps. 141:8): "Bring my soul out of prison, that it may confess Your name."[35] Therefore, having refuted these, we say with Aristotle in *On the Causes of the Properties of the Elements and Planets, II* that when the water of a man falls into the womb of a woman, it is boiled in that strong decoction and becomes a piece of flesh, and a soul is created in it by the command of God.

(1,4) What, therefore, Plato says that the seed of souls is in the stars, was said by reason of analogy, which is in the proportion of the human intellect to the intellect of celestial intelligence. Nor do the stars come forth except to minister, as the god of gods himself says, that he himself makes the seed of these. For this is not in the power of the seed, which is before the act, but is the constitutional action of the intellect.

(2) Yet, Ovid's saying is metaphorical, since it is only through the white path of innocence and sloth that we arrive "at the great thundering roofs."

(3) In regard to what is objected to by reason, we must say that those of whom there is only one essential act from equality, that their nature is one. Now to understand and to contemplate intellectually is not from the equality of celestial intelligence and from the rational soul, but through all things, before and after. For the understanding of intelligence is without continuity, time, and without integration, and is in the very first truth of all things. Yet, our understanding is with the continuity of time, having itself relate to the first truths of things, just as the eye of a bat to the light of the sun. Thus, by prior and posterior, it is possible to understand having a higher and lower nature, which differ in their specificity.

Regarding what the Commentator said, we must say that continuation is not according to a single, common nature, but

---

[35] This is actually Psalm 142:7

according to one, common object of speculation. Pertaining to the happiness that is after death, as Aristotle said in the *Book of Heaven and the World*[36], that outside heaven there is neither time nor place, but only a happy life, and an understanding that there is something beyond heaven, that which is above the course of the stars, in the place of the quiet contemplation of the blessed.

---

[36] Perhaps better known under the title 'On the Heavens'. Its Latin title is extended to the title familiar to Albert (*De Caelo et Mundo*).

Latin Text

Quaeritur de fato, an sit, quid sit, utrum neccessitatem imponat rebus et an scibile sit et in quo genere causae incidat.

Art. I. An fatum sit

Ad primum obicitur sic:

(1) Nihil diffinitur, nisi quod habet esse; fatum a Boethio diffinitur in IV De Consolatione Philosophiae; ergo habet esse.

(2) Item, in II De generatione dicit Aristoteles, quod unumquodque mensuratur periodo; mensura autem per aliquid sui minimum, iteratum super quantitatem mensurati, certificat et numerat quantitatem ipsius. Si ergo vita et esse inferiorum mensura circuli, quae vocatur periodus, mensuratur, est accipere in mensura circuli aliquam partem, quae per se vel aequale sibi esse et vitam inferiorum numerando certificat. Per gradus ergo circuli distinctos secundum duodecim domos certificatur esse et vita inferiorum. Non autem accipitur periodus sine contentis in periodo planetis et stellis et his quae accidunt eis ex situ et radiatione. Igitur ex stellis caelestis et radiatione et situ earum scitur et numeratur omne esse et vita et partes esse et vitae inferiorum; hoc autem fatum vocatur; ergo fatum habet esse.

(3) Item, dicit Aristoteles in IV Physicorum, quod esse in tempore est a quadam parte temporis mensurari. Tempus autem, cum unum sit numero et non multiplicetur per multitudinem temporalium, oportet, quod per unum aliquid ad durationem temporalium omnium referatur. Hoc autem non est nisi motus circuli caelestis. Ergo per motum circuli caelestis causatur et numeratur esse et vita omnium inferiorum; et hoc fatum vocatur; ergo fatum est; "motus" enim circuli, ut dicit Aristoteles, est "tamquam vita existentibus omnibus".

(4) Si forte dicatur, quod ex motu caelesti inhaeret dispositio quaedam inferioribus, sed haec vincitur a qualitatibus materiae et sic excluditur, contra: inferiores causae, quae sunt in materia, ordinatae sunt ad superiores sicut materialia ad sua formalia et sicut locata ad sua loca et sicut mota ad sua moventia; ergo superiora informant, continent et movent inferiora. Informantia autem, continentia et moventia semper vincunt; ergo omne esse et vita inferiorum vincitur et trahitur ad dispositionem superiorum.

(5) Si dicas, quod verum est quantum ad corpora, sicut videtur Augustinus dicere in V De civitate dei, quod "afflatus sidereos" possumus dicere valere usque ad corpum transmutationes, non autem ad animae, contra: vires animae vegetabilis et sensibilis non operantur extra sui organi harmoniam; si ergo harmonia regatur afflatibus sidereis, per consequens et operationes animae sensibilis et vegetabilis afflatibus sidereis regulabuntur.

(6) Ulterius etiam hoc videtur de anima rationali, quia dicit Philosophus, quod intellectus noster est cum continuo et tempore. Temporalia autem et continua sensu et imaginatione percipiuntur; habitum autem est iam, quod talia subiacent afflatibus sidereis, ergo per consequens et operationes intellectus.

(7) Item, dicit Philosophus, quod anima est instrumentum inteligentiae et quod intelligentia imprimit in eam et illuminat eam; ergo intelligentia movendo causat formas illuminationis in anima intellectuali. Sed inter movens et motum non est medium, ut probat Aristoteles in VII Physicorum; ergo intelligentia sic movens erit immediata animae; aut ergo est immediata per seipsam aut per aliquod medium deferens causalitatem suam ad animam. Non per seipsam, quia philosophice loquendo intelligentia est motor orbis. Oportet ergo, quod medium sit, quod deferat illuminationes eius ad animam. Medium autem hoc non potest accipi nisi motus caeli influens per motum inferioribus formas motoris. Ergo intelligentia per motum caeli regulat et causat operationes intellectualis animae.

Hoc per simile videre possumus; cor enim, quod secundum Aristotelem "est principium vitae et vegetationis et sensus", membris distantibus a se virtutes has non influit nisi per vehiculum spiritus; et sic est in omnibus moventibus et motis, quae distant ab invicem. Similiter igitur erit in intelligentia et anima, quando intelligentia distat et imprimit in animam rationalem, secundum locum distans ab ea. Non enim philosophice dici potest, quod intelligentia veniat inferius, quia secundum Philosophum intelligentia in orbe est et numeratur ad numerum orbium vel ad numerum motuum orbis, et ipse orbis motus, sicut dicit Aristoteles, componitur ex intelligentia movente et circulo caelesti, qui movetur.

(8) Item, somnia, ex quibus pronosticantur futura, ut dicit Macrobius, sive sint oracula sive intelligentiae sive prophetiae, sunt in nobis tripliciter, sicut dicit Aristoteles in II De somno et vigilia, scilicet per signum vel per causam vel per accidens; quod, inquam, accidens causae per se, non accidens communiter. Est autem somnium passio somni; ergo per aliquid dormitionis, accidit somnium dormienti. Accidens autem dormitionis quod est pronosticum futuri, non potest causari a calido et humido, frigido et sicco, quae sunt in materia. Oportet ergo, quod causetur a forma aliqua, quae est forma ordinis et regula vitae inferiorum; et haec forma non potest esse nisi a circulo caelesti. Ergo per circulum caelestem aliquid adhaeret inferioribus, per quod regulatur tota vitae dispositio; et hoc fatum vocatur; ergo fatum est.

(9) Item, Ptolemaeus dicit, quod elector melius pronosticatur, qui signa futurorum accipit a stellis secundis, stellas secundas vocans effectus stellarum, qui apparent in inferioribus elementis, sicut in nubibus vel aliquo huiusmodi; ex hoc habetur, quod effectus stellarum adhaerent inferioribus, ex quibus futura dispositio vitae et esse causatur et noscitur. Hoc autem fatum vocant mathematici; ergo fatum est.

(10) Item, Boethius in V De consolatione philosophae loquitur de casu et fortuna, quae causantur ex duabus causis per se concurrentibus, sicut quando aliquis intendit suffodere thesaurum et postea alius in eodem loco intendit fodere sepulcrum, consequitur ex fortuna inventio thesauri, et sic fortuna causatur ex duabus causis per se concurrentibus, ut dicit Boethius; has autem "causas concurrere facit ordo ille inevitabili conexione" causarum, qui "de fonte praescientiae procedit": conexio autem huiusmodi causarum a Boethius fatum vocatur; ergo fatum est.

(11) Item, Boethius ibidem: Quae summa praevidit providentiae simplicitas, "fatum singula digerit in motum locis, formilis, temporibusque distributa"; ergo fatum est.

(12) Si dicas, quod fatum est ordo praescientiae divinae, hoc non repugnat his quae dicta sunt, quoniam praescientia divina ea quae praeordinavit, exsequitur et administrat ministerio causarum naturalium, et explicitus ordo esse et vitae ab huismodi causis fatum vocatur.

Contra:
(13) dicit Gregorius in Homilia de epiphania Domini: "Absit a fidelium cordibus, ut fatum aliquid esse credatur", et reddit rationem: "quoniam stellae factae sunt propter hominem, non homo propter stellas". Si ergo stellarum motus esset ratio vitae hominis, minister regularet vitam domini, cui ministrat; quod est inconveniens.

(14) Item, Augustinus in libro De doctrina christiana fatum dicit nihil esse; et si mathematici aliquando vera de futuris praenuntiare videntur, dicit hoc fieri operatione daemonum ad deceptionem infidelium.

(15) Item, si est fatum, aut est causa causatum. Non causatum, quia hoc regulatur fato, ut dicunt mathematici; ergo erit causa. Si causa,

aut inferior aut superior: non inferior, quia illae sunt calidum, frigidum, humidum et siccum, quorum nullum est fatum, nec superior, quia causa superior est circulus caelestis cum suo motu, quod mathematici non dicunt esse fatum, sed causam fati; ergo fatum nihil est.

(16) Item, res non habent nisi duplex esse, ut dicit Augustinus, scilicet in causa prima, in qua sunt vita et lux, quorum neutrum est fatum, et in seipsis; sed nec esse rei in seipsa est fatum, ut dicunt mathematici, sed potius regulatum a fato; ergo fatum nihil est.

(17) Item, Augustinus dicit, quod inferiorum sufficit dicere voluntatem Dei esse causam, quia omnia fiunt vel deo volente vel Deo permittente; voluntas autem dei non est fatum; ergo ipsum nihil est.

(18) Item, omne quod habet esse, tenet ordinem, ut dicit Boethius: sed fatum non tenet ordinem, quia videmus indignos exaltari et dignos deici, quod inordinatum est; cum igitur fatum circa talia esse ponatur, fatum nihil esse videtur.

(19) Item, si fatum est effectus circuli caelestis, ea quae sunt unius circuli, videntur esse unius fati; sed Iacob et Esau, "ex uno concubitu Isaac, patris nostri", concepti, unius sunt circuli, et tamen non fuerunt unius fati, sicut consequens probavit eventus; ergo videtur fatum nihil esse.

Art. 2. Quid sit fatum

Ulterius quaeritur, quid sit fatum.

(20) Et dicit Boethius IV De consolatione philosophiae, quod "fatum est inhaerens rebus mobilibus dispositio, per quam providentia suis quaeque nectit ordinibus".

(21) Hermes autem Trismegistus dicit, quod fatum, quod Graeci ymarmenen dicunt, est causarum complexio singulis temporaliter distribuens, quae sacramento deorum caelestium sunt praeordinata.

Solutio:
Fatum multipliciter dicitur. Fatum aliquando dicitur mors dispositione periodi inducta, sicut dicitur in Anticludiano: "Livor post fata quiescit". Hoc enim modo decursum vitae tribus fatalibus deabus attribuit Plato, inceptionem scilicet Clotho et Lachesi progressum et conclusionem termini Atropo, sicut dicitur: "Clotho colum baiulat, Lachesis trahit, Atropos occat". Et hoc modo non quaeritur hic de fato.

(20) Secundo modo dicitur fatum dispositio providentiae divinae de futuro progressu esse et vitae inferiorum. Quae dispositio cum sit aeterna, constat, quod nihil ponit in rebus, sed cum explicatur in effectu, tunc effectus ille per res digeritur et expletur temporibus et locis opportunis, sicut etiam praeordinatio et praedeterminatio alicuius in mente de gerendis negotiis suis per aliquem nuntium nihil ponit in nuntio, sed tamen per nuntium expletur, quando nuntium dirigit et negotia sibi iniungit; et hoc modo Boethius in "[De] Consolatione philosophiae" loquitur de fato. Et hoc modo iterum non quaeritur hic de fato. Forma tamen huius praeordinationis in mente divina existens simplex est et divina et aeterna et immaterialis et incommutabilis, et tamen cum per res temporales explicatur, temporalis fit et materialis et multiplicata, mobilis et contingens.

(21) Tertio modo dicitur fatum forma ordinis esse et vitae inferiorum, causata in ipsis ex periodo caelestis circuli, qui suis radiationibus ambit nativitates eorum; et hoc modo Hermes loquitur de fato, deos vocans stellas et sacramentum deorum immobilem dispositionem esse et vitae inferiorum. Est autem haec forma non forma dans esse, sed potius forma cuiusdam universalis ordinis esse et vitae, simplex in essentia, multiplex in virtute; et simplicitatem essentiae habet a simplicitate circulationis circuli communis, multiplicitatem autem virtutis habet a multitudine eorum quae continentur in circulo. Fluit enim a multis stellis et sitibus et imaginibus et radiationibus et coniunctionibus et praeventionibus et multiplicibus angulis, qui describuntur ex intersecationibus radiorum caelestium corporum et productione radiorum super centrum, in quo solo, sicut dicit Ptolemaeus, omnes virtutes eorum quae sunt in caelesti circulo, congregantur et adunantur. Haec autem talis forma media est inter necessarium et possibile; necessarium enim est, quidquid est in motu caelestis circuli, possibile autem et mutabile, quidquid est in materia generabilium et corruptibilium. Forma autem ista causata ex caelesti circulo et inhaerens generabilibus et corruptibilibus, media est inter utrumque. Omne enim quod procedit a causa nobili in causatum ignobile, licet in aliquo teneat proprietatem causae, tamen esse suum non est, nisi quantum permittit possibilitas subiecti, in quo est; omne enim quod recipitur, ut dicunt Boethius et Aristoteles in VI Ethicorum, est in eo in quo recipitur, secundum potestatem recipientis et non secundum potestatem causae, a qua est. Hoc possumus videre in his quae a Dionysio dicuntur processiones divinae, sicut est vita et ratio et sapientia et huiusmodi, quae secundum quod procedunt longius a deo secundum gradus entium, efficiuntur magis temporalia et mutabilia et potentiae materiali et privationi permixta, cum tamen in deo sint simplicissima et aeterna et immutabilia et immaterialia. Et similiter est de forma ordinis esse et vitae, quae in caelesti circulo est necessaria et immutabilis, hoc est inalterabilis, in rebus vero generatis propter mutabilitatem esse

ipsarum est recepta contingenter et mutabiliter. Unde Boethius in De consolatione philosophiae figurat multos circulos, in quorum centro cardo et causa est fati et fatalium. Et in circulo primo propinquo centro est immutabilitas fati, secundum quod refertur ad causam, et in circulo distante, in quo continentur generabilia et corruptibilia eiusdem fati, est contingentia et mutabilitas per esse generatorum et corruptorum. Et sic centrum est dispositio esse et vitae in mente motoris primi; circulus iuxta centrum propinquus est eadem forma dispositionis, prout est in periodo caelesti, circulus autem a centro distans designat eandem formam dispositionis, prout mutabiliter adhaeret rebus generatis et corruptis. Forma autem haec, cum sit imago periodi, potentialiter et virtualiter praehabet totum esse et operationem durationis generatorum et corruptorum; et sic, licet sit ex necessario, tamen est mutabilis et contingens. Cuius causam optime assignat Ptolemaeus in Quadripartito, dicens, quod virtutes stellarum per aliud et per accidens fiunt in inferioribus, per aliud quidem, quia per sphaeram activorum et passivorum, per quorum qualitates activas et passivas inhaerent inferioribus; per accidens autem, quia cum haec forma effluat a causa neccessaria et immutabili, accidit ei habere esse in rebus contingentibus et mutabilibus. Ex duobus ergo habet mutabilitatem, scilicet exqualitatibus elementorum, per quas defertur ad generata, et ex esse generatorum, in quo est sicut in subiecto. Hoc igitur est fatum.

(1) Et sic primae rationi consentimus; concedimus enim, quod hoc modo esse habet.

(2) Et hoc modo secundam rationem concedimus, quod quae sunt, mensurantur periodo.

(3,4) Ad id autem quod tertio obicitur et quarto, dicimus, quod inferiora quidem nata sunt oboedire superioribus, sed inferius et superius dupliciter referuntur ad invicem. Si enim relatio fiat per unam et simplicem formam, quam dat superior et accipit inferior motor, verum est, quod superiori movente de necessitate movetur inferior; et talis forte relatio est inter motores superiores et inferiores orbium caelestium. Si autem inferior motor sit in forma una, quam non accipit a superiori, sed refertur ad ipsum sicut directus ab ipso et instrumentum eius, nihil prohibet, quin per contrarium suae formae vel aliam dispositionem ad aliud inclinantem impediatur, ita quod a superiori motum non suscipit; et sic est de calido et frigido relatis ad virtutes caelestium; calidum enim per propriam formam, non caelestem, est congregativum homogeneorum et disgregativum heterogeneorum, et frigidum e contrario. Et ideo istae qualitates, per contrarietatem inventam in materia et diversitatem dispositionum materiae saepe excludunt effectus motus caelestis. Propter quod Ptolemaeus dicit, quod sapiens homo dominatur astris; ubi dicit Commentator, quod si effectus circuli caelestis minorando humores corpora disponit ad quartanam, sapiens medicus hoc praevidens per calida et humida corpora disponit ad sanguinem et tunc excluso effectu caelesti quartana non inducitur.

1. Ad id quod obicitur ulterius, respondendum est, quod hoc modo ad fatum referuntur operationes virtutum vegetabilium et sensibilium. Cum tamen dispositio fatalis exclusibilis sit et impedibilis ab oppositis dispositionibus inventis in materia, exclusibilis etiam est ab oppositis dispositionibus inventis in anima sensibili. Hoc enim faciunt apprehensa in virtutibus animae sensibilis, quod faciunt dispositiones activarum et passivarum qualitatum in corporibus; unde imaginatione mulieris concepta, totum corpus transmutatur ad venerea. Propter quod etiam Avicenna dicit, quod quidam ex imaginatione leprae leprosus factus est, et patientibus fluxum sanguinis prohibet Galenus aspectum rubicundorum. Si igitur apprehensa sint contraria motui caelesti, excludunt effectum eius, sicut per contrarias dispositiones excluditur a corpore. Per convenientes autem motui caelesti dispositiones corporales et apprehensiones animales iuvatur caelestis effectus. Et hoc est quod dicit Messehallach, quod

caelestis effectus, quem ille alatir vocat, iuvatur a sapiente astronomo, sicut in producendis terraenascentibus iuvatur aratione et seminatione.

(8) Ad hoc quod obicitur de causa somniorum, de plano videtur mihi esse concedendum, maxime de somniis, quae fiunt per imaginarias visiones.

(7) Ad hoc quod obicitur de illuminatione intellectus animae rationalis, secundum philosophiam dupliciter respondetur: Uno modo secundum Stoicos, qui ponunt, quod omnis substantia nobilior per imperium habet movere inferiorem et inferior oboedit ei, sicut in fascinationibus anima unius videndo alterum impedit et ligat operationes eius; dicunt enim, quod virtute alicuius naturae superioris, sive intelligentiae sive stellae, anima unius ponitur in gradu superiori et alterius in inferiori, et tunc inferior nata est mutari ab apprehensione superioris, et sic fieri fascinationem, et quod dicit Aristoteles, quod inter movens et motum non est medium, non dicunt intelligi semper de immediatione loci sive spatii, sed de immediatione gradus superioris et inferioris, ponentes exemplum de eo quod prius inductum est, quia organum imaginationis non est immediatum vasis seminariis et tamen imagine mulieris concepta extenduntur vasa seminaria et affluit semen propter immediationem superioritatis et inferioritatis, quae est inter praecipiens et id cui praecipitur. Hoc autem secundum sententiam Peripateticorum non bene convenit, quia sine dubio inter agens et movens et motum immediatio debet esse coniunctionis et contactus. Propter quod dicimus, quod sicut calor digestivus duplicis est virtutis et unam virtutem habet, inquantum est calor ignis secundum se consideratus, quae est alterare et separare ea quae sunt diversi generis, et decoquere, alteram habet, inquantum est instrumentum animae, quae est principium vitae, secundum quam terminat digerendo ad formam vivi, ita etiam caelestis motus duplicis est virtutis: uno modo, prout est motus corporis orbicularis, et sic movet corpora; alio modo, prout est

instrumentum intelligentiae moventis et hoc modo effectus eius efficitur in anima sensibili per formas corporum et in anima intellectuali per formas illuminationum, quia, sicut diximus, formae, quae fiunt in aliquo, fiunt in ipso secundum potestatem recipientis et non secundum potestatem dantis.

Quaecumque alia ad hanc partem obiecta sunt, plana sunt.

(13) Ad dictum Gregorii dicendum est, quod ipse loquitur de fato, secundum quod a quibusdam philosophis et haereticis necessitatem rebus imponere dicebatur, secundum quod dicit poeta de Paride:

"Te tua fata trahunt, ne coepta relinquere possis".

(15) Ad hoc quod quaeritur, utrum fatum sit causa vel causatum, dicendum, quod est similitudo causae universi ordinis vitae et esse, et sic est aliquid causae, licet non sit vera causa. Et secundum quod adhaeret rebus generatis, est dispositio causata, licet causae similitudinem exprimat; est enim forma continens decursum esse et vitae mobiliter et contingenter.

(19) Ad hoc quod obicitur de geminis, dicendum, quod licet possemus dicere, quod in uno concubitu semen per vices proicitur et per vices a matrice glutitur, et sic non esse unam horam conceptus geminorum, tamen etiamsi demus <eos> in una hora concipi, centrum tamen cordis eorum, a quo incipit conceptus formari, non est unum; et mutato centro necesse est mutari totum circulum, et sic horizon eorum non est unus, neque anguli sunt iidem nec eadem domorum dispositio. Et sic tota periodus efficitur diversa, et per consequens adhaerens rebus natis dispositio fatalis necessario variatur.

Et per hoc patet solutio ad ea quae quaesita sunt de hoc articulo.

(16-18) Alia sunt levia et per se patentia unicuique.

Art. 3. Utrum necessitatem rebus imponat

Consequenter quaeritur, utrum fatum necessitatem rebus imponat.

(1) Et videtur, quod sic. Cuius enim causa necessaria est, ipsum etiam necessarium est; causa autem fati est caelestis circulus, qui necessarius est; ergo et fatum est necessarium et necessitatem rebus imponit.

(2) Item, fatum est mensura et regula totius esse et vitae; regulatum autem necessario refertur ad regulam; sed regula est necessaria; ergo videtur, quod fatum rebus fatalibus imponat necessitatem.

(3) Item, fortiora sunt superiora quam inferiora; ergo superiora ad sui dispositionem necessario trahunt inferiora; cum autem fatum sit vinculum, per quod inferiora trahuntur ad superiora, videbitur fatum necessitatem imponere rebus.

(4) Item, Aristoteles dicit, quod inter moventia superiora et inferiora concors est harmonia sicut in concordis citharae; sed ad harmoniam necessarium est, quod inferiora per omnia consequantur dispositionem superiorum; ergo dispositio superiorum adhaerens inferioribus necessitatem imponit eis.

Contra:
Fatum est adhaerens rebus mobilibus, ut supra dictum est, et per mobiles res adveniens; sed motis mobilibus moventur ea quae in ipsis sunt: ergo fatum est dispositio in diversa mutabilis; contingenter igitur se habet ad res et non imponit necessitatem.

Solutio:
Dicendum, quod fatum mutatur multiplici de causa, sicut superius diximus; et ideo nullam necessitatem imponit rebus, sed inclinat ad effectus caelestium, si non sit opposita dispositio fortior in materia in contrarium movens. Et indeo huiusmodi moventia assimilat

Aristoteles in II De somno et vigilia duplicibus consiliariis; sapientes enim consiliarii ex rationibus certis suadent aliquid utiliter esse faciendum, quod tamen inferiores propter adversos casis obviantes dissuadent, et tunc solvitur lex consilii sapientum. Et est suum verbum tale, quod saepe supervenientibus aliis consiliis consilia mutantur sapientum; regula enim, ut dicit Aristoteles Lesbiae aedificationis mutatur ad aedificatum. Est autem Lesbia insula, in qua lapides non ad rectam lineam sunt dolabiles, et ideo oportet, quod regula, secundum quam dolantur, aliquantulum curvetur ad ipsas aedificationes. Et ita est de dispositione esse et vitae inferiorum, in qua propter causas, quae sunt in materia, saepe mutatur dispositio sapiens circuli caelestis, et ipsa dispositio adhaerens mobilibus, quae fatum vocatur, extra rectitudinem caelestium declinans exorbitat propter multas oppositas inferiorum transmutationes.

(1) Ad primum ergo dicendum, quod causa fati neccessaria est; sed ex hoc non sequitur, nisi quod sit ipsum neccessarium esse, sed non sequitur ulterius, quod neccessitatem imponat rebus, quia non inhaeret eis secundum potestatem caelestium, quae neccessaria sunt, sed secundum potestatem inferiorum, quae omnino mutabilia et contingentia sunt.

(2) Ad secundum dicendum, quod relatio, quae est inter regulans et regulatum, neccesaria est sicut relatio, quae est inter patrem et filium. Sed quia mutatio causat relationem et causat relationis destructionem, ideo mutatio, quae est in rebus mobilibus, causa est, quod regulatum non sequitur regulam [et non sequitur ad ipsam], et quoad hoc est non regulatum.

(3) Ad tertium dicendum, quod licet fortiora sint superioria quam inferioria, tamen ex impotentia inferiorum contingit, quod non omnia possunt assequi superiorum effectus, et quoad hoc ex parte ipsorum solvitur vinculum.

(4) Ad quartum dicendum, quod solutio temperantiae chordarum dissonantiam inducit in cithara; et similiter mutatio et alteratio inferiorum dissonantiam facit ab effectu superiorum; unde dicit Damascenus, quod superiora inferiorum quaedam sunt signa, nostrorum autem actuum nullo modo sunt causa.

Art. 4. An fatum sit scibile

Consequenter quaeritur, an fatum sit scibile.

(1) Et videtur, quod non; cum enim sit effectus caelestis circuli et similitudo quaedam ipsius, sicut forma ordinis alicuius similis est ipsi causae ordinis eiusdem – et in caelesti circulo quoad nos infinita consideranda sunt, sicut stellae in numero et specie et virtutibus et situs earum in circulo declivi et extra ipsum et distantiae et coniunctiones et quantitas anguli, sub quo indicit radius, et pars fortunae et gradus lucidi et umbrosi in puteis et in turribus existentes et huiusmodi infinita quoad nos, videbitur etiam, quod effectus eius a nobis sciri non possit.

(2) Item, circulus continet datorem vitae et datorem fortunae et datorem sensus et intellectus, qui hyleg et alchochoden a matemathicis vocantur; aliter enim non esset mensura totius vitae, quia principium vitae non includeret; hora enim principii omnium horarum est hora enim principii omnium horarum est hora casus seminis in matricem. Hanc autem quoad nos non contingit scire. Ergo ignorabitur forma dispositionis totius vitae, et sic ignorata erit fatalis dispositio rerum.

(3) Et hoc videtur ex effectibus. Sunt enim quaedam, quorum videtur esse una periodus, et tamen accidentia eorum per se, sicut est sexus masculinus et femininus, non sunt eadem, et causam huius non contingit scire ex caelestis circuli effectu.

(4) Similiter est, quod natus in octavo mense moritur ut frequentius et natus in septimo vivit.

(5) Similiter in geminis, quorum unus est masculus et alter femina, rarissime contingit masculum vivere, femina autem aliquando supervivit; et causam horum aut impossibile aut valde difficile est assignare ex caelesti circulo.

(6) Item, quod luminaribus existentibus in capite Algol sive Gorgonis, si ea Mars respectu inimicitiae radiaverit, natus, ut dicit Ptolemaeus, truncabitur manibus et pedibus, et truncatus suspendetur in cruce.

(7) Item, de hoc quod dicit, quod luna in Leone existente vestimenta nova ne induas, difficile est valde causam invenire ex caelesti circulo, et si huiusmodi conclusiones essent scibiles, essent ad haec principia ex quibus via syllogistica concluderentur, ordinata. Nunc nulla via rationis videtur esse; non enim sequitur: Luna est in Leone, ergo malum est induere vestes novas. Aut: luminaria sunt in capite Gorgonis, et respicit ea inimica radiatio Martis a quadrato vel ab opposita diametro; ergo natus tunc suspendetur in cruce.

Solutio:
Dicendum, quod duae partes sunt astronomiae, sicut dicit Ptolemaeus: una est de sitibus superiorum et quantitatibus eorum et passionibus propriis; et ad hanc per demonstrationem pervenitur. Alia est de effectibus astrorum in inferioribus, qui in rebus mutabilibus mutabiliter recipiuntur; et ideo ad hanc non pervenitur nisi per coniecturam, et oportet astronomum in ista parte secundum aliquid physicum esse et ex signis physicis coniecturari. Coniecturatio autem, cum sit ex signis mutabilibus, generat habitum minoris certitudinis, quam sit scientia vel opinio. Cum enim huiusmodi signa sint communia et mutabilia, non potest haberi ex ipsis via syllogistica, eo quod nec in omnibus nec in pluribus includunt significatum, sed quantum est de se, sunt iudicia quaedam multis de causis mutabilia, sicut patet per antedicta. Et ideo saepe astronomus dicit verum et tamen non evenit, quod dicit, quia dictum suum fuit quoad dispositionem caelestium verissimum, sed haec dispositio a mutabilitate inferiorum exlusa est.

(1) Ad primum dicendum, quod quidem multa et quoad nos infinita consideranda essent, sed considerantur paucissima, quibus oboediunt alia, et ex illis pronosticabilis habetur coniecturatio. Propter hoc dicit Ptolemaeus, quod elector non nisi probabiliter et communiter iudicare debet, hoc est per causas superiores communes, quas propriae rerum causae frequentissime excludunt.

(2) Ad aliud dicendum, quod hora talis difficulter scitur, et ideo inventum est remedium, ut accipiatur ascendens gradus occulti, hoc est horae coniunctionis vel praeventionis luminarium adaequatur circulus, quia ille habet influentiam ad omnem nativitatem, quae proximo sequitur; vel accipiatur ascendens ad nativitatem ex utero.

(3) Ad aliud dicendum, quod via syllogistica sciri non potest conclusio coniecturalis; sed tamen imperfectio scientiae non impedit, ut dicit Ptolemaeus, quin hoc inde sciatur, quod inde sciri potest, sicut etiam est in pronosticatione somniorum. Non enim habitudo syllogistica est inter imaginem somnialem et interpretationem somnii; et sic est in omnibus existimationibus coniecturalibus.

(5) Ad hoc quod quaeritur de disparitate sexus in geminis, dicendum, quod sexus femineus semper fit per occasionem defectus alicuius principiorum. Cum enim semen masculi factivum sit et formativum per virtutem formativam, quam habet in semetipso, semper inducit formam masculi de intentione propria, nisi qualitate materiae impediatur, et ideo sexus femineus indicit ex defectu, nec natura particularis unquam intendit facere feminam; sed cum melius fieri non possit ex natura universali, fit adiutorium generationis et non generans proprie; et haec est femina. Et hoc est, quod intendit dominus dicere Gen. II, 18: "Non est", inquit, "bonum hominem", hoc est virum, "esse solum; faciamus ei adiutorium simile sibi". Unde dispar sexus in geminis provenit ex defectu principiorum naturalium in altera parte seminis et non ex periodo caelesti. Quod autem in talibus geminis mas ut frequentius

moritur, contingit ex hoc quod cum tales gemini ex uno semine diviso generentur, fuit materia male terminabilis a virtute formativa, quia si bene fuisset terminabilis, utrumque formasset in marem. Materia autem masculi maiori et meliori indiget terminatione quam materia feminae, et ideo masculus remanet aegrotus et debilis et ex interminatione quam materia feminae, materiae causam mortis habens, femina autem, cui parva sufficit terminatio, propter mollitiem corporis aius aliquando supervivit; frequentissime tamen ambo moriuntur.

(4) Ad hoc quod obicitur de octavo mense, falso dixerunt quidam, quod ut frequentius octavo mense natus moritur, quia octavus mensis Saturno attribuitur, cuius frigus et siccitas natum interficiunt. Hoc enim falsum probatur per hoc quod multi in astronomia filii Saturni esse dicuntur, qui diu supervivunt. Causa ergo non est in caelesti circulo, sed in principiis naturae. Luna enim est magis dominativa, ad cuius conversiones mensurantur conceptus et impraegnationes, ut dicit Aristoteles. Luna enim est alter sol, eo quod lumen a sole recipit, et quod sol facit in anno, luna facit in mense. A prima enim incensione usque ad hoc quod est dimidia, est calida et humida sicut vernum tempus; a mediatione usque ad plenilunium est calida et sicca sicut aestas; a plenilunio usque ad secundam mediationem est frigida et sicca sicut autumnus; a seconda meditatione usque ad coniunctionem est frigida et humida sicut hiems. Quod autem nata sit movere humorem, patet in accessu et recessu maris, qui accessus et recesus maris in media lunatione, quae est quattuordecim dierum, ad circulum in descendendo et ascendendo. Si enim minimus sit fluxus maris, ad idem punctum parvitatis revertetur die quarta decima. Licet enim luna in media lunatione non transeat nisi medietatem circuli sui, tamen motus augis ex opposito occurrens sibi complet aliam circuli medietatem. Luna enim in quolibet mense bis est in auge, scilicet in praeventione et coniunctione cum sole. Luna enim in coniunctione vivificum lumen a sole accipit, et cum Venus numquam longe distet a sole et Venus habeat movere humorem

seminalem, luna quando soli coniungitur, acquirit Veneris virtutem. Et sic ex virtute propria movet humorem, ex virtute solis influit vitam humori moto et ex virtute Veneris movet seminis genituram ad formas geniturae convenientes. Et quia Mercurius etiam est cum sole, Mercurius habet commiscibilem virtutem ex multis gyrationibus eius, quas habet super omnem alium planetam, et luna hanc virtutem meretur ex coniunctione ad ipsum, et ex illa coniunctione semen viri et feminae movet in commixtionem. Sic ergo luna conversionibus suis commixtiones, conceptus et impraegnationes causat et regulat. Sunt autem in genitura septem mutationes necessariae. Quarum prima est seminis conversio, et praecipue ad formam cordis, ad quam totum aliud formatur. Secunda est materiae distinctio ad formam membrorum principalium, quae et creatrices habent virtutes, sicut hepar creat virtutes naturales et cerebrum virtutes animales et vasa seminaria virtutes formativas conceptuum. Et ideo in secunda mutatione adhaerent puncto cordis tres vesiculae, quas facit spiritus delatus ad locum cerebri, hepatis et vasorum seminalium. Tertia mutatio est distinctio materiae, quando vesicula cerebri ascendit sursum et vesicula hepatis aliquantulum inferius ad dextrum, et ad ultimum descendit vesica vasorum seminalium; et hunc descensum et ascensum facit exsufflatio spiritus, qui est in corde. Quarta mutatio est totius materiae distinctio, ut distribuatur locis membrorum secundariorum, quae creatrices virtutes non habent: et hanc distinctionem iterum facit cordis exsufflatio. Quae exsufflatio et perforat et distendit materiam et perforando quidem facit vias venarum pulsatilium et quietarum et nervorum, extendendo autem distribuit uniuscuiusque membri materiam in locum proprium. Quinta mutatio est transmutatio materiae in figuram membrorum, quam figuram non reciperet nisi esset humida et hanc mutationem facit vis formativa cordis vecta in locum membrorum per spiritum exsufflatum. Membra autem figurata non sunt apta recipere virtutem motivam et operativam nisi per consolidationem et colligationem, quae sexta mutatione complentur per calorem cordis cum spiritu diffusum in membra, qui exsiccans superfluum

humidum consolidat et confortat iuncturas et conexiones. Septima
mutatione motus per virtutes motivas omnibus membris a corde in
fluitur. Et cum omnis motus geniturae sit a luna, sicut iam dictum
est, oportet, quod septem conversionibus lunae in homine, quod
est animal perffectissimum, compleatur. Et licet istae mutationes
seminis non fiant successive secundum numerum mensium, tamen
perfectio earum non fit nisi completo numero conversionum
secundum septem menses. Et in animalibus aliis ab homine non
haec ita regulariter observantur propter ignobilitatem suarum
complexionum, sed alia diutius ut elephas, alia breviori tempore
impraegnantur. Perfectis autem his septem conversionibus seminis
embryo habet ea quae ad necessitatem exiguntur. Sed, sicut dicit
Galenus, virtus formativa tripliciter se habet ad materiam;
aliquando enim materia est diminuta et virtus abundans, aliquando
sunt secundum aequalitatem proportionata, aliquando virtus est
deficiens et materia superabundans. Et quando quidem virtus est
abundans et materia diminuta, terminata est completo septimo
mense; et tunc virtus abundans fortem facit motum ad exitum, et
nascitur puer et convalescit et efficitur parvus corpore et agillis
valde in operationibus. Quando autem sunt adaequata virtus et
materia et quando est superabundans materia, tunc non est
completa septimo mense, sed quiescit per unam lunae
conversionem, quae est mensis octavus, et completa terminatione
in nono mense facit motum ad exitum et nascitur nono mense et
convalescit; et haec est ut in pluribus fere omnium nativitas. Si
autem est virtus deficiens ex inoboediantia materiae, ex angustia
facit motum in septimo mense, quando virtus motiva data est, et ex
defectu non complet ipsum nisi mense octavo, et tunc nascitur et
moritur ut in pluribus; et hoc non contingit ex periodo, sed ex
corruptionem pricipiorum naturalium. Haec autem quae dicta sunt,
ut in pluribus sunt vera; multum enim variationis faciunt
complexiones feminarum et complexiones climatum. Propter quod
ego vidi unam, quae peperit in undecimo mense puerum maximae
quantitatis; et Aristoteles dicit se vidisse unam, quae peperit in
mense decimo quarto.

(6) Ad hoc quod obicitur de nato in capite Gorgonis, dicendum quod illae stellae funerae sunt et monstruosam indicant vitae terminationem; propter quod etiam ipse Perseus hoc caput averso vultu abscisum tenet. Sed hoc sicut primo diximus, necessitatem rebus non imponit, sed facile mutabilem inclinationem.

(7) Et idem modus solutionis est de nova veste induta, luna existentem in Leone; sicut enim radiatio periodi dispositionem ordinis esse et durationis imprimit rebus naturalibus, ita imprimit artificiatis.

(8) Propter quod figurae imaginum magicarum ad aspectum stellarum fieri praecipiuntur.

Art. 5. In quo genere causae fatum incidat

Quod autem quaeritur, in quo genere causae incidat, iam solutum est per antecedentia, quoniam in veritate causa non est, sed est aliquid causae; est enim forma ordinis esse et vitae, imaginem habens virtutum caelestis circuli, sicut etiam dicimus aliquando, quod aliqua non vere sunt entia neque non entia, sed sunt aliqud entis, sicut ea quae sunt in anima, et secundum aliquos motus et tempus, ut dicit Avicenna.

(1) Quidam tamen nituntur probare, quod sit causa, eo quod Plato ponit compares stellas his quae nascuntur, in quibus sunt formae, quae sunt causae rerum generatarum et regula esse et vitae earum. Inducit enim deum deorum loquentem ad deos corporales, qui sunt stellae, et dicentem: "Horum", idest generatorum in inferioribus, "sementem ego faciam vobisque tradam; vestrum erit par exsequi". Et praecipit eis quod simile sibi viderent in natura et pietatem colere et iustitiam diligere, quod "hoc" ad se sumant post nexus terreni dissolutionem, intelligens "hoc" de hominibus piis, quorum immortalis et intellectus et post mortem sidereas sedes accipiens, sicut a semente siderum in generationem descendit. Propter quod etiam dixit, quod descendens per circulos planetarum vires animae accipit, memoriam, inteligentiam et voluntatem et huiusmodi, sicut exponit Macrobius "Super somnium Scipionis".

(2) Hoc etiam videtur tangere Ovidius loquens de lacteo circulo et dicens: "Hac iter est superis ad magni tecta tonantis".

(3) Hoc etiam videtur per rationem, quia quorum est unus essentialis actus, illorum videtur esse una natura; intelligentiae autem caelestis et intelligentiae hominis in conceptione veri videtur esse unus essentialis actus, ergo una natura.

(4) Inde ulterius: Quarumcumque formarum est una natura, illarum una relatio est ad corpus unius naturae, si in aliquo corpore esse

dicantur; sed intelligentiae caelestis relatio est ad stellam vel ad orbem comparem sibi; ergo et intellectualis naturae in homine erit relatio ad stellam comparem.

(5) Hoc etiam videtur per dictum Commentatoris super XI Metaphysicae, ubi dicit quod finis prosperitatis intellectus hominis est, si post mortem continuetur motori caelesti.

Solutio:

Dicendum, quod falsum et haereticum est dicere quod animae intellectuales descendant a compare stella; Aegyptiorum enim philosophorum haec fuit opinio, quod intellectuales animae in stellis a deo deorum factae, terreno affectu, quo aliquando afficiuntur, gravantur et illa gravitate deprimuntur ad corpora generabilia et corruptibilia et eodem depuratae per cultum pietatis et iustitiae recipiuntur ad stellas compares. Affectum autem terrenum ad intellectuales animas pervenire dixerunt eo modo quo afficitur anima circa dulcedinem nutrimenti corporis. Posuerunt enim quod subtilissimo vapore paludum Maeotidarum inter duos solstitiales positarum, inter quos maximus discursus planetarum est, nutriuntur corpora planetarum, ita quod quando illum attrahunt ex gravitate deprimuntur et retrogradandur, et quando eundem digerunt, elevantur et cursu diriguuntur; hunc autem subtiliatum in sphaera ignis et aëris necta deorum vocabant. Et hoc modo affectum terrenorum ad animas in stellis positas pervenire dixerunt. Haeretici autem ab hac opinione occasionem erroris sumentes, dixerunt animas omnes in caelo cum angelis factas propter peccatum, quod ibi commiserunt, in corpora ista terrena esse detrusas, ut hic purificatae iterum ad caelestes sedes recipiantur, et hoc esse quod dicit David (PS. CXLI, 8): "Educ de carcere animam meam ut confiteatur nomini tuo". His ergo refutatis dicimus cum Aristotele in II De causis proprietatum elementorum et planetarum, quod cum cadit aqua viri in matricem mulieris, decoquitur in ea decoctione forti et fit frustum carnis, et creatur in eo anima iussu Dei.

(1,4) Quod ergo dicit Plato sementem animarum esse in stellis, ratione similitudinis, quae est in proportione intellectus humani ad intellectum inteligentiae caelestis, dictum est; nec stellae ex equuntur nisi per ministerium, sicut et ipse deus deorum dicit, quod ipse horum sementem facit; sementis enim haec non est in potentia, quae sit ante actum, sed est ipsa actio naturae intellectualis.

(2) Dictum autem Ovidii metaphoricum est, quoniam non nisi per viam candidam candore innocentiae et institiae pervenitur "ad magni tecta tonantis".

(3) Ad illud quod obicitur per rationem, dicendum, quod quorum ex aequo est unus essentialis actus, illorum est una natura. Intelligere autem et contemplari intellectualiter non ex aequo est intelligentiae caelestis et animae rationalis, sed per prius et posterius, quia intellectus intelligentiae est sine continuo et tempore et sine collatione et in ipsa prima rerum veritate, intellectus autem noster est cum continuo et tempore, habens se ad primas rerum veritates sicut oculus vespertilionis ad lucem solis. Sic autem per prius et posterius habere intelligere contingit ex superiori et inferiori natura, quae specifice differunt.

Ad dictum Commentatoris dicendum, quod continuatio non est secundum unam et communem naturam, sed secundum unum et commune obiectum speculationis ad beatitudinem, quae post mortem est, pertinentis, sicut dicit Aristoteles in Libro de caelo et mundo, quod extra caelum non est tempus nec locus, sed vita beata, intelligens extra caelum esse quod est supra cursum siderum in loco quietae contemplationis beatorum.